Collected
Poems and Epigrams

COLLECTED
POEMS and EPIGRAMS

J. V. CUNNINGHAM

FABER AND FABER
3 Queen Square London

First published in 1971
by Faber and Faber Limited
3 Queen Square London W.C.1
Printed in Great Britain by
The Bowering Press Plymouth
All rights reserved

ISBN 0 571 09284 5

Most of the poems in this collection were first published in the author's *The Helmsman* (San Francisco, 1942), *The Judge is Fury* (New York, 1947), *Doctor Drink* (Cummington, Mass., 1950), *The Quest of the Opal* (Denver, 1950), The Augustan Reprint Society pamphlet, number 24 (Los Angeles, 1950), *The Exclusions of a Rhyme* (Denver, 1960), *To What Strangers, What Welcome* (Denver, 1964), and *Some Salt* ([Madison], 1967). Many had serial publication in the following magazines, broadsides and anthologies: *Commonweal, Hound and Horn, New York Times, The Magazine, Modern Verse, Trial Balances* (New York, 1936), *Twelve Poets of the Pacific* (Norfolk, Conn., 1937), *New Mexico Quarterly Review, Arizona Quarterly, Poetry, Philological Quarterly, New Poems by American Poets* (New York, 1953), *Poems in Folio* (San Francisco, 1957), *Partisan Review, Carleton Miscellany, Latin Lines* ([Detroit], 1965), *Denver Quarterly, Southern Review*, and *New American Review*.

Contents

POEMS

Poems I
1931-1934

The Phoenix

More than the ash stays you from nothingness!
Nor here nor there is a consuming pyre!
Your essence is in infinite regress
That burns with varying consistent fire,
Mythical bird that bears in burying!

I have not found you in exhausted breath
That carves its image on the Northern air,
I have not found you on the glass of death
Though I am told that I shall find you there,
Imperturbable in the final cold,

There where the North wind shapes white cenotaphs,
There where snowdrifts cover the fathers' mound,
Unmarked but for these wintry epitaphs,
Still are you singing there without sound,
Your mute voice on the crystal embers flinging.

Lector Aere Perennior

Poets survive in fame.
But how can substance trade
The body for a name
Wherewith no soul's arrayed?

No form inspires the clay
Now breathless of what was
Save the imputed sway
Of some Pythagoras,

Some man so deftly mad
His metamorphosed shade,
Leaving the flesh it had,
Breathes on the words they made.

The Wandering Scholar's Prayer
to St. Catherine of Egypt

Past ruined cities down the grass,
Past wayside smokers in the shade,
Clicking their heels the fruit cars pass
Old stations where the night is stayed.

Curved on the racking wheel's retreat,
Sweet Catherine, rise from time to come,
Number in pain the fruit car fleet,
And throw confusion in the sum!

The vagrants smoke in solitude,
Sick of the spittle without cough;
Not unabsolved do they grow rude,
Dying with Swift in idiot froth.

From revery, sweet saint, forfend
Those ravelled faces of the park!
When questing cars at twilight's end
Cozen the eyes with chilling dark,

Save them from memory of the light,
The circuit of the orient sun
Wheeling loud silence through the night
Like headlamps where the twin rails run.

The Dogdays

hic in reducta valle Caniculae
vitabis aestus . . .

The morning changes in the sun
As though the hush were insecure,
And love, so perilously begun,
Could never in the noon endure,

The noon of unachieved intent,
Grown hazy with unshadowed light,
Where changing is subservient
To hope no longer, nor delight.

Nothing alive will stir for hours,
Dispassion will leave love unsaid,
While through the window masked with flowers
A lone wasp staggers from the dead.

Watch now, bereft of coming days,
The wasp in the darkened chamber fly,
Whirring ever in an airy maze,
Lost in the light he entered by.

Elegy for a Cricket

at vobis male sit, malae tenebrae
Orci, quae omnia bella devoratis!

Fifteen nights I have lain awake and called you
But you walk ever on and give no answer:
Therefore, damned by my sole, go down to hellfire.
Spirit luminous and footstep uncertain,
You will pace off forever the halls of great Dis.
You there, caught in the whirling throng of lovers,
If you find in that fire her whom I loved once,
Say to her that I gave you few but true words.
Say to her that your dream as her dream held me,
Alone, waking, until your friend, the cock, slept.
Say to her, if she ask what shoe you wear now,
That I gave you my last, I have none other.

All Choice is Error

This dry and lusty wind has stirred all night
The tossing forest of one sleepless tree,
And I in waking vision walked with her
Whose hair hums to the motion of the forest
And in the orbit of whose eyelids' fall
The clouds drift slowly from the starry wharves.
I knew her body well but could not speak,
For comprehension is a kind of silence,
The last harmonic of all sound. Europa,
Iö, and Danäe: their names are love
Incarnate in the chronicles of love.
I trace their sad initials which thy bark,
Gaunt tree, may line with age but not efface,
And carve her name with mine there. The tree is gnarled
And puckered as a child that looks away
And fumbles at the breast—prodigious infant
Still sucking at the haggard teats of time,
Radical change, the root of human woe!

All choice is error, the tragical mistake,
And you are mine because I name you mine.
Kiss, then, in pledge of the imponderables
That tilt the balance of eternity
A leaf's weight up and down. Though we must part
While each dawn darkens on the fortunate wheel,
The moon will not soften our names cut here
Till every sheltering bird has fled the nest.

They know the wind brings rain, and rain and wind
Will smooth the outlines of our lettering
To the simplicity of epitaph.

Obsequies for a Poetess

The candles gutter in her quiet room,
And retrospect, returning through the sad
Degrees of dusk that had o'ershadowed pain,
Finds her Lethean source, the unmemoried stream
Of cold sensation. There, vain Sibylls clothed
In solemn ash, their hair dishevelled, weep
The close of centuries where time like stanzas
Stands in division, disposed, and none
Dare chant antiphonal to that strain. Pale Aubrey
Finds there his faint and final rest; there Dowson
Pillows his fond head on each breast. For them
And their compeers, our blind and exiled ghosts
Which nightly gull us with oblivion,
Weave we this garland of deciduous bloom
With subtle thorn. Their verse, sepulchral, breathes
A careless scent of flowers in late July,
Too brief for pleasure, though its pleasure lie
In skilled inconscience of its brevity.

In Innocence

In innocence I said,
'Affection is secure.
It is not forced or led.'
No longer sure

Of the least certainty
I have erased the mind,
As mendicants who see
Mimic the blind.

Noon

I have heard the self's stir,
Anonymous
And low, as on the stair
At time of Angelus

The worshippers repeat
An exorcism,
The angled clock's repute
Conjured with chrism.

Distinctions at Dusk

Closed in a final rain
Clouds are complete,
Vows of shadowful light
Are vain,
And every hour is late.

Pride is a sky ingrown,
Selfishly fond,
By the edged sun nor found
Nor known,
But in the dusk defined.

Ripeness is All

Let us not live with Lear,
Not ever at extremes
Of ecstasy and fear,
Joy in what only seems,
Rage in the madman's hut
Or on the thunderous hill,
Crying *To kill, to kill!*
Nor in a blind desire
To sire we know not what
Ravish the eternal Will.

The Scarecrow

His speech is spare,
An orchard scare
With battered hat;
Face rude and flat,
Whose painted eye
Jove's flashing doom
From broken sky
Can scarce illume:
The Thunderer
May strike his ear,
And no reply.

Hymn in Adversity

Fickle mankind!
When force and change
Wildly derange
The casual mind
   On chance begotten,

Trust in the Lord,
For that is best.
As for the rest,
Though not ignored
   And not forgotten,

The heart not whole
Nor quite at ease,
Here finds some peace,
Some wealth of soul,
   Albeit ill-gotten.

A Moral Poem

Then leave old regret,
Ancestral remorse,
Which, though you forget,
Unseen keep their course;

Shaping what each says,
Weathered in his style,
They in his fond ways
Live on for a while.

But leave them at last
To find their own home.
Inured to the past,
Be what you become:

Nor ungrudgingly
The young hours dispense,
Nor live curiously,
Cheating providence.

Fancy

Keep the quick eyes hid in the mind!
Unleash them when the game is spied!
Free-reined fancy will but make blind
Your carnal soul, flesh glorified.

But firm fancy, untimely stayed,
Fixed on the one shape, still rehearsed,
Becomes the idol that it made,
Possessed by pure matter, accursed.

The hot flesh and passionless mind
In fancy's house must still abide,
Each share the work, its share defined
By caution under custom's guide.

The Symposium

Over the heady wine,
Well-watered with good sense,
Come sing the simple line
And charm confusion hence.

The fathers on the shelves
Surely approve our toasts,
Surely are here themselves,
Warm, amiable ghosts,

Glad to escape the new
Regenerate elect
Who take the social view
And zealously reject

The classic indignation,
The sullen clarity
Of passions in their station,
Moved by propriety.

The Beacon

Men give their hearts away;
Whether for good or ill
    They cannot say
Who shape the object in their will.

The will in pure delight
Conceives itself. I praise
    Far lamps at night,
Cold landmarks for reflection's gaze.

Distant they still remain,
Oh, unassailed, apart!
    May time attain
The promise ere death seals the heart!

The Chase

The rabbit crossed and dodged and turned;
I'd swear she neither saw nor heard
But ran for pleasure, unconcerned,
Erratic as a garden bird,

Timid and shy, but not afraid.
Say that her life was in the chase,
Yet it was nothing that God made
But wild blood glorying in a race

Through the cornfields of the lower Kaw.
My horse was tired before she fell.
Love does not work by natural law,
But as it is it's just as well,

For when the dogs retreated, fought,
And circled the embarrassed doe,
The doe moved only to be caught,
Self-pleased to be encircled so.

And I sat still, gun at my side.
Esteem and wonder stayed desire.
The kill is down. Time will abide.
Time to remember and inquire.

The Helmsman: An Ode

The voyage of the soul is simply
   Through age to wisdom;
      But wisdom, if it comes,
Comes like the ripening gleam of wheat,

Nourished by comfort, care, rain, sunlight,
   And briefly shining
      On windy and hot days,
Flashing like snakes underneath the haze.

But this, a memory of childhood,
   Of loves forgotten,
      And they who gave are still,
Gone now, irrevocable, undone.

O Penury, steadied to your will,
   I tread my own path,
      Though Self-Respect, discreet,
Plucks at my arm as I pass down street,

Querulous and pert. They tell in story
   That for proud Ajax,
      Vaingloriously self-slain,
Teucer set forth from his friends and kin;

He on the western shore of parting
   Paused to address them:
      'Comrades who have with me
Countless misfortunes endured, O mine!

Brave friends, banish tonight dark sorrow;
   Set the white tables
      With garlands, lamps, with wine;
Drink and, tomorrow, untravelled seas!'

So sailed guileful Odysseus, so sailed
   Pious Aeneas,
      And cloudless skies brought sleep,
Stilling th' unmasterable, surging deep,

The helmsman stilled, his sea-craft guiding.
   O too confiding
      In star and wind and wave,
Naked you lie in an unknown grave.

Poems II
1935-1941

Coffee

When I awoke with cold
And looked for you, my dear,
And the dusk inward rolled,
Not light or dark, but drear,

Unabsolute, unshaped,
That no glass can oppose,
I fled not to escape
Myself, but to transpose.

I have so often fled
Wherever I could drink
Dark coffee and there read
More than a man would think

That I say I waste time
For contemplation's sake:
In an uncumbered clime
Minute inductions wake,

Insight flows in my pen.
I know nor fear nor haste.
Time is my own again.
I waste it for the waste.

To a Friend, on her Examination for the Doctorate in English

After these years of lectures heard,
Of papers read, of hopes deferred,
Of days spent in the dark stacks
In learning the impervious facts
So well you can dispense with them,
Now that the final day has come
When you shall answer name and date
Where fool and scholar judge your fate
What have you gained?
                              A learnèd grace
And lines of knowledge on the face,
A spirit weary but composed
By true perceptions well-disposed,
A soft voice and historic phrase
Sounding the speech of Tudor days,
What ignorance cannot assail
Or daily novelty amaze,
Knowledge enforced by firm detail.

What revels will these trials entail,
What gentle wine confuse your head
While gossip lingers on the dead
Till all the questions wash away,
For you have learned, not what to say,
But how the saying must be said.

The Metaphysical Amorist

You are the problem I propose,
My dear, the text my musings glose:
I call you for convenience love.
By definition you're a cause
Inferred by necessary laws—
You are so to the saints above.
But in this shadowy lower life
I sleep with a terrestrial wife
And earthy children I beget.
Love is a fiction I must use,
A privilege I can abuse,
And sometimes something I forget.

Now, in the heavenly other place
Love is in the eternal mind
The luminous form whose shade she is,
A ghost discarnate, thought defined.
She was so to my early bliss,
She is so while I comprehend
The forms my senses apprehend,
And in the end she will be so.

Her whom my hands embrace I kiss,
Her whom my mind infers I know.
The one exists in time and space
And as she was she will not be;
The other is in her own grace
And is *She is* eternally.

Plato! you shall not plague my life.
I married a terrestrial wife.
And Hume! she is not mere sensation
In sequence of observed relation.
She has two forms—ah, thank you, Duns!—,
I know her in both ways at once.
I knew her, yes, before I knew her,
And by both means I must construe her,
And none among you shall undo her.

For My Contemporaries

How time reverses
The proud in heart!
I now make verses
Who aimed at art.

But I sleep well.
Ambitious boys
Whose big lines swell
With spiritual noise,

Despise me not,
And be not queasy
To praise somewhat:
Verse is not easy.

But rage who will.
Time that procured me
Good sense and skill
Of madness cured me.

Timor Dei

Most beautiful, most dear,
When I would use Thy light,
Beloved, omniscient Seer,
Thou didst abuse my sight;

Thou didst pervade my being
Like marsh air steeped in brine;
Thou didst invade my seeing
Till all I saw was Thine.

Today, from my own fence
I saw the grass fires rise,
And saw Thine old incense
Borne up in frosty sighs.

Most terrible, most rude,
I will not shed a tear
For lost beatitude,
But I still fear Thy fear.

Choice

Allegiance is assigned
Forever when the mind
Chooses and stamps the will.
Thus, I must love you still
Through good and ill.

But though we cannot part
We may retract the heart
And build such privacies
As self-regard agrees
Conduce to ease.

So manners will repair
The ravage of despair
Which generous love invites,
Preferring quiet nights
To vain delights.

Summer Idyll

There is a kind of privacy,
Immobile as the windless wheat,
Within whose dusty seignory
We ripen with maturing heat.

Dreamless repose, unvisioned rest,
Gold harvest that we will not reap,
Perfect the sleeper on your breast!
And if he wake not? He will sleep.

August Hail

In late summer the wild geese
In the white draws are flying.
The grain beards in the blue peace.
The weeds are drying.

The hushed sky breeds hail.
Who shall revenge unreason?
Wheat headless in the white flail
Denies the season.

This Tower of Sun

There is no stillness in this wood.
The quiet of this clearing
Is the denial of my hearing
The sounds I should.

There is no vision in this glade.
This tower of sun revealing
The timbered scaffoldage is stealing
Essence from shade.

Only my love is love's ideal.
The love I could discover
In these recesses knows no lover,
Is the unreal,

The undefined, unanalysed,
Unabsolute many;
It is antithesis of any,
In none comprised.

Autumn

Gather the heart! The leaves
Fall in the red day. Grieves
No man more than the season.
Indifference is my guide.

Heart mellow and hope whirling
In a wild autumn hurling
Is time, and not time's treason.
And fatigue is my bride.

But say what moralist
Shall in himself subsist?
The tried. And you, occasion,
Far in my heart shall hide.

I have watched trains recede
Into that distance. Heed,
O heed not their persuasion
Who in no lands abide!

Passion

Passion is never fact
And never in a kiss,
For it is pure unact,
All other than the this.

It is love's negative,
Love's furious potency,
Distinct from which we live
In the affirmed to be.

And as love's passive form
Is not this form I see
But all the loves that swarm
In the unwilled to be,

So in this actual kiss,
Unfaithful, I am true:
I realize in this
All passion, act, and you.

Reason and Nature

This pool in a pure frame,
This mirror of the vision of my name,
    Is a fiction
On the unrippled surface of reflection.

I see a willowed pool
Where the flies skim. Its angles have no rule.
    In no facet
Is the full vision imaged or implicit.

I've heard, in such a place
Narcissus sought the vision of his face.
    If the water
Concealed it, could he, drowning, see it better?

I know both what I see
And what I think, to alter and to be,
    And the vision
Of this informs that vision of confusion.

L'Esprit de Géometrie et L'Esprit de Finesse

In anima hominis dominatur violentia rationis.
St Bonaventure

*Qui ne sait que la vue de chats, de rats, l'écrasement d'un charbon, etc.,
emportent la raison hors des gonds?*
Pascal

    Yes, we are all
    By sense or thought
      Distraught.
The violence of reason rules
    The subtle Schools;
A falling ember has unhinged Pascal.

    I know such men
    Of wild perceptions.
      Conceptions
Cold as the serpent and as wise
    Have held my eyes:
Their fierce impersonal forms have moved my pen.

Montana Pastoral

I am no shepherd of a child's surmises.
I have seen fear where the coiled serpent rises,

Thirst where the grasses burn in early May
And thistle, mustard, and the wild oat stay.

There is dust in this air. I saw in the heat
Grasshoppers busy in the threshing wheat.

So to this hour. Through the warm dusk I drove
To blizzards sifting on the hissing stove,

And found no images of pastoral will,
But fear, thirst, hunger, and this huddled chill.

Poems III

1942-1947

Envoi

Hear me, whom I betrayed
While in this spell I stayed,
Anger, cathartic aid,
Hear and approve my song!

See from this sheltered cove
The symbol of my spell
Calm for adventure move,
Wild in repose of love,
Sea-going on a shell
In a moist dream. How long—
Time to which years are vain—
I on this coastal plain,
Rain and rank weed, raw air,
Served that fey despair,
Far from the lands I knew!

Winds of my country blew
Not with such motion—keen,
Stinging, and I as lean,
Savage, direct, and bitten,
Not pitying and unclean.

Anger, my ode is written.

Not for Charity

What is it to forgive?
It is not to forget,
To forfeit memory
   In which I live.
It is to be in debt
To those who injure me.

If then I shall forgive
And consciously resign
My claim in love's estate
   In which I live,
Know that the choice is mine
And is the same as hate.

Say then that I forgive.
I choose indignity
In which my passions burn
   While I shall live,
O not for Charity,
But for my old concern.

The Predestined Space

Simplicity assuages
With grace the damaged heart,
So would I in these pages
If will were art.

But the best engineer
Of metre, rhyme, and thought
Can only tool each gear
To what he sought

If chance with craft combines
In the predestined space
To lend his damaged lines
Redeeming grace.

Acknowledgement

Your book affords
The peace of art,
Within whose boards
The passive heart

Impassive sleeps,
And like pressed flowers,
Though scentless, keeps
The scented hours.

The Man of Feeling

The music of your feeling has its form,
And its symphonic solitude affirms
The resonance of self, remote and warm,
With private acmes at appointed terms.

So yours, so mine. And no one overhears.
O sealed composer of an endless past,
Rejoice that in that harmony of spheres
Pythagoras and Protagoras fuse at last!

The Solipsist

There is no moral treason;
Others are you. Your *hence*
Is personal consequence;
Desire is reason.

There is no moral strife.
None falls in the abysm
Who dwells there, solipsism
His way of life.

Fear

Love, at what distance mine!
On whose disdain I dine
Unfed, unfamished, I
In your hid counsels lie.
I know your lover, fear.
His presence is austere
As winter air. He trembles
Though the taut face dissembles.
I know him: I am he.

Convalescence

I found that consciousness itself betrays
Silence, the fever of my harried days.

In the last circle of infirmity
Where I almost attained simplicity—

So to recite as if it were not said,
So to renounce as if one lost instead—

My unabandoned soul withdrew abhorred.
I knew oblivion was its own reward,

But pride is life, and I had longed for death
Only in consciousness of indrawn breath.

Ars Amoris

Speak to her heart.
That manic force
When wits depart
Forbids remorse.

Dream with her dreaming
Until her lust
Seems to her seeming
An act of trust.

Do without doing.
Love's wilful potion
Veils the ensuing,
And brief, commotion.

Meditation on Statistical Method

Plato, despair!
We prove by norms
How numbers bear
Empiric forms,

How random wrong
Will average right
If time be long
And error slight;

But in our hearts
Hyperbole
Curves and departs
To infinity.

Error is boundless.
Nor hope nor doubt,
Though both be groundless,
Will average out.

Meditation on a Memoir

Who knows his will?
Who knows what mood
His hours fulfil?
His griefs conclude?

Surf of illusion
Spins from the deep
And skilled delusion
Sustains his sleep.

When silence hears
In its delight
The tide of tears
In the salt night,

And stirs, and tenses,
Who knows what themes,
What lunar senses,
Compel his dreams?

To the Reader

Time will assuage.
Time's verses bury
Margin and page
In commentary,

For gloss demands
A gloss annexed
Till busy hands
Blot out the text,

And all's coherent.
Search in this gloss
No text inherent:
The text was loss.

The gain is gloss.

With a copy of Swift's Works

Underneath this pretty cover
Lies Vanessa's, Stella's lover.
You that undertake this story
For his life nor death be sorry
Who the Absolute so loved
Motion to its zero moved,
Till, immobile in that chill,
Fury hardened in the will,
And the trivial, bestial flesh
In its jacket ceased to thresh,
And the soul none dare forgive
Quiet lay, and ceased to live.

Haecceity

Evil is any this or this
Pursued beyond hypothesis.

It is the scribbling of affection
On the blank pages of perfection.

Evil is presentness bereaved
Of all the futures it conceived,

Wilful and realized restriction
Of the insatiate forms of fiction.

It is this poem, or this act.
It is this absolute of fact.

Agnosco Veteris Vestigia Flammae

I have been here. Dispersed in meditation,
I sense the traces of the old surmise—
Passion dense as fatigue, faithful as pain,
As joy foreboding. O my void, my being
In the suspended sources of experience,
Massive in promise, unhistorical
Being of unbeing, of all futures full,
Unrealized in none, how love betrays you,
Turns you to process and a fluid fact
Whose future specifies its past, whose past
Precedes it, and whose history is its being.

To My Daimon

Self-knower, self-aware,
Accomplice in despair,

Silence and shade increase
In corridors of peace

Till in a chapeled prayer
Warm grace wells from despair—

But if my heart offend me,
Daimon, can you defend me?

Who know myself within
The sinner and the sin.

Distraction

I have distracted time.
In a full day your face
Has only its own place.
Tired from irrelevance
I sleep, and dream by chance,
Till passion can exact
No faith, and fails in act,
Till timelessness recedes
Beneath the apparent needs
Of a distracted time.

Poems IV
1948-1968

In the Thirtieth Year

In the thirtieth year of life
I took my heart to be my wife,

And as I turn in bed by night
I have my heart for my delight.

No other heart may mine estrange
For my heart changes as I change,

And it is bound, and I am free,
And with my death it dies with me.

An Interview with Doctor Drink

I have a fifth of therapy
In the house, and transference there.
Doctor, there's not much wrong with me,
Only a sick rattlesnake somewhere

In the house, if it be there at all,
But the lithe mouth is coiled. The shapes
Of door and window move. I call.
What is it that pulls down the drapes,

Disheveled and exposed? Your rye
Twists in my throat: intimacy
Is like hard liquor. Who but I
Coil there and squat, and pay your fee?

The Aged Lover Discourses in the Flat Style

There are, perhaps, whom passion gives a grace,
Who fuse and part as dancers on the stage,
But that is not for me, not at my age,
Not with my bony shoulders and fat face.
Yet in my clumsiness I found a place
And use for passion: with it I ignore
My gaucheries and yours, and feel no more
The awkwardness of the absurd embrace.

It is a pact men make, and seal in flesh,
To be so busy with their own desires
Their loves may be as busy with their own,
And not in union. Though the two enmesh
Like gears in motion, each with each conspires
To be at once together and alone.

I, too, have been to the Huntington

A railroad baron in the West
Built this nest,

With someone else's pick and shovel
Built this hovel,

And bought these statues semi-nude,
Semi-lewd,

Where ladies' bosoms are revealed,
And concealed,

And David equally with Venus
Has no penis.

The True Religion

The New Religion is the True,
A transformation overdue,
A thorough Freudly Reformation
Based like the old on a translation.
Their fear is our anxiety,
Our complex their humility.
The virtuous are now repressed,
The penitent are now depressed,
Even the elect are simply manic,
And chastity is pansy-panic.

In brief, the Convert is a Case.
He puts away all else to face
Reality with the paralysis
Of a seven year depth analysis.
He does not see but he is heard.
He is transferred and untransferred.
He has aggressions and no malice,
And phallic symbols and no phallus.

Horoscope

Out of one's birth
The magi chart his worth;
They mark the influence
Of hour and day, and weigh what thence

Will come to be.
I in their cold sky see
Neither Venus nor Mars;
It is the past that cast the stars

That guide me now.
In winter when the bough
Has lost its leaves, the storm
That piled them deep will keep them warm.

To my Wife

And does the heart grow old? You know
In the indiscriminate green
Of summer or in earliest snow
A landscape is another scene,

Inchoate and anonymous,
And every rock and bush and drift
As our affections alter us
Will alter with the season's shift.

So love by love we come at last,
As through the exclusions of a rhyme,
Or the exactions of a past,
To the simplicity of time,

The antiquity of grace, where yet
We live in terror and delight
With love as quiet as regret
And love like anger in the night.

Monday Morning

The flattery has been infrequent
And somewhat grudging. There is junk mail
And no letter. The weather cloudy
With more snow. Fortuitous meeting,
The rustle of flirtation, the look—
Self-esteem sustained by any excuse,
By any misconstruction? No. No.
It is now a January world,
An after Christmas waiting. For what?
Not for this snow, this silence. There is
No resonance in the universe.
I must buy something extra today
And clutter up my house and my life.

Consolatio Nova

For Alan Swallow

To speak of death is to deny it, is
To give unpredicated substance phrase
And being. So the discontinuous,
The present instant absent finally
Without future or past, is yet in time
For we are time, monads of purposes
Beyond ourselves that are not purposes,
A causeless all of momentary somes.
And in such fiction we can think of death.

Think

Let us forget praise and blame,
Speak only of quietness
And survival. Mad toadstools
Grow in the dampness, englobed
Enormities, inherited
Treachery of all our pasts.
Forget. What was day is night.
In curtained sufficiency
Rest in the living silence,
Rest in arrogant sleep. Think
What houseflies have died in time.

Montana Fifty Years Ago

Gaunt kept house with her child for the old man,
Met at the train, dust-driven as the sink
She came to, the child white as the alkali.
To the West distant mountains, the Big Lake
To the Northeast. Dead trees and almost dead
In the front yard, the front door locked and nailed,
A handpump in the sink. Outside, a land
Of gophers, cottontails, and rattlesnakes,
In good years of alfalfa, oats, and wheat.
Root cellar, blacksmith shop, milk house, and barn,
Granary, corral. An old *World Almanac*
To thumb at night, the child coughing, the lamp smoked,
The chores done. So he came to her one night,
To the front room, now bedroom, and moved in.
Nothing was said, nothing was ever said.
And then the child died and she disappeared.
This was Montana fifty years ago.

To What Strangers, What Welcome

a sequence of short poems

I

I drive Westward. Tumble and loco weed
Persist. And in the vacancies of need,
The leisure of desire, whirlwinds a face
As luminous as love, lost as this place.

2

On either side of the white line
The emblems of a life appear
In turn: purpose like lodgepole pine
Competitive and thin, and fear

Agile as aspen in a storm.
And then the twilit harboring
In a small park. The room is warm.
And by the ache of travelling

Removed from all immediacy,
From all time, I as time grows late
Sense in disordered fantasy
The sound and smell of love and hate.

3

In a few days now when two memories meet
In that place of disease, waste, and desire
Where forms receptive, featureless, and vast
Find occupation, in that narrow dark,
That warm sweat of a carnal tenderness,
What figure in the pantheon of lust,
What demon is our god? What name subsumes
That act external to our sleeping selves?
Not pleasure—it is much too broad and narrow—,
Not sex, not for the moment love, but pride,
And not in prowess, but pride undefined,
Autonomous in its unthought demands,
A bit of vanity, but mostly pride.

4

You have here no otherness,
Unadressed correspondent,
No gaunt clavicles, no hair
Of bushy intimacy.
You are not, and I write here
The name of no signature
To the unsaid—a letter
At midnight, a memorial
And occupation of time.

I'll not summon you, or feel
In the alert dream the give
And stay of flesh, the tactile
Conspiracy.
                    The snow falls
With its inveterate meaning,
And I follow the barbed wire
To trough, to barn, to the house,
To what strangers, what welcome
In the late blizzard of time.

On the highway cars flashing,
Occasional and random
As pain gone without symptom,
And fear drifts with the North wind.
We neither give nor receive:

The unfinishable drink
Left on the table, the sleep
Alcoholic and final
In the mute exile of time.

5

The soft lights, the companionship, the beers,
And night promises everything you lacked.
The short drive, the unmade bed, and night in tears
Hysteric in the elemental act.

6

It was in Vegas. Celibate and able
I left the silver dollars on the table
And tried the show. The black-out, baggy pants,
Of course, and then this answer to romance:
Her ass twitching as if it had the fits,
Her gold crotch grinding, her athletic tits,
One clock, the other counter clockwise twirling.
It was enough to stop a man from girling.

7

A traveller, the highway my guide,
And a little bastard of a dog
My friend. I have pin-ups for passion
As I go moseying about these scenes,
Myself improbable as yucca,
Illusory as the bright desert,
And finally here: the surf breaking,
Repetitive and varied as love
Enacted, and inevitably
The last rim of sunset on the sea.

8

The night is still. The unfailing surf
In passion and subsidence moves
As at a distance. The glass walls,
And redwood, are my utmost being.
And is there there in the last shadow,
There in the final privacies
Of unaccosted grace,—is there,
Gracing the tedium to death,
An intimation? Something much
Like love, like loneliness adrowse
In states more primitive than peace,
In the warm wonder of winter sun.

9

Innocent to innocent,
One asked, What is perfect love?
Not knowing it is not love,
Which is imperfect—some kind
Of love or other, some kind
Of interchange with wanting,
There when all else is wanting,
Something by which we make do.

So, impaired, uninnocent,
If I love you—as I do—
To the very perfection
Of perfect imperfection,
It's that I care more for you
Than for my feeling for you.

10

A half hour for coffee, and at night
An hour or so of unspoken speech,
Hemming a summer dress as the tide
Turns at the right time.
                                 Must it be sin,
This consummation of who knows what?
This sharp cry at entrance, once, and twice?
This unfulfilled fulfilment?
                                 Something
That happens because it must happen.
We live in the given. Consequence,
And lack of consequence, both fail us.
Good is what we can do with evil.

11

I drive Eastward. The ethics of return,
Like the night sound of coyotes on a hill
Heard in eroded canyons of concern,
Disposes what has happened, and what will.

Absence, my angel, presence at my side,
I know you as an article of faith
By desert, prairie, and this stonewalled road—
As much my own as is the thought of death.

The once hooked ever after lives in lack,
And the once said never finds its way back.

I write only to say this,
In a syllabic dryness
As inglorious as I feel:
Sometime before drinking time
For the first time in some weeks
I heard of you, the casual
News of a new life, silence
Of unconfronted feeling
And maples in the slant sun
The gay colour of decay.
Was it unforgivable,
My darling, that you loved me?

Identity, that spectator
Of what he calls himself, that net
And aggregate of energies
In transient combination—some
So marginal are they mine? Or is
There mine? I sit in the last warmth
Of a New England fall, and I?
A premise of identity
Where the lost hurries to be lost,
Both in its own best interests
And in the interests of life.

A Century of Epigrams

1 An old dissembler who lived out his lie
   Lies here as if he did not fear to die.

With a book of clavier music

2 Discursive sense, unthought, unclear,
   Is in this music planned;
   Error is not of nature here
   But of the human hand.

With a Detective Story

3 Old friend, you'll know by this how scholars live:
   The scholar is a mere conservative,
   A man whose being is in what is not,
   The proud tradition and the poisoned plot.
   He is bewildered in the things that were,
   He thrives on sherry and the murderer,
   And with his bottle on a rainy night
   By Aristotle's saws brings crimes to light.
       So with this murderer may you make merry
       And we'll redeem him with a glass of sherry.

4 Jove courted Danäe with golden love,
   But you're not Danäe, and I'm not Jove.

The Lover's Ghost Returns to the Underworld

5 Farewell, false love! Dawn and Lethean doom
   Recall me. Where I go you too must come.
   Others possess you here: there, mine alone,
   You will sleep with me, grinding bone to bone.

6   I don't know what I am. I think I know
    Much of the circumstance in which I flow.
    But knowledge is not power; I am that flow
    Of history and of percept which I know.

7   All hastens to its end. If life and love
    Seem slow it is their ends we're ignorant of.

8   In whose will is our peace? Thou happiness,
    Thou ghostly promise, to thee I confess
    Neither in thine nor love's nor in that form
    Disquiet hints at have I yet been warm;
    And if I rest not till I rest in thee
    Cold as thy grace, whose hand shall comfort me?

9   Deep sowing of our shame, rage of our need,
    Gross shadow of Idea, impersonal seed,
    Unclothed desire! the malice of your thrust
    Is his to use who takes his love on trust.

10 If wisdom, as it seems it is,
    Be the recovery of some bliss
    From the conditions of disaster—
    Terror the servant, man the master—
    It does not follow we should seek
    Crises to prove ourselves unweak.
    Much of our lives, God knows, is error,
    But who will trifle with unrest?

These fools who would solicit terror,
Obsessed with being unobsessed,
Professionals of experience
Who have disasters to withstand them
As if fear never had unmanned them,
Flaunt a presumptuous innocence.

I have preferred indifference.

I I Homer was poor. His scholars live at ease,
Making as many Homers as you please,
And every Homer furnishes a book.
Though guests be parasitic on the cook
The moral is: *It is the guest who dines.*
I'll write a book to prove I wrote these lines.

I 2 Time heals not: it extends a sorrow's scope
As goldsmiths gold, which we may wear like hope.

Epigraph to The Helmsman

I 3 Of thirty years ten years I gave to rhyme
That that time should not pass: so passes time.

On the cover of my first book

I 4 This garish and red cover made me start.
I who amused myself with quietness
Am here discovered. In this flowery dress
I read the wild wallpaper of my heart.

15 Deep summer, and time pauses. Sorrow wastes
To a new sorrow. While time heals time hastes.

16 The dry soul rages. The unfeeling feel
With the dry vehemence of the unreal.
So I in the Idea of your arms, unwon,
Am as the real in the unreal undone.

17 What is this visage? in what fears arrayed?
This ghost I conjured though that ghost was laid?
The vision of a vision still unstayed
By my voice, still by its own fears dismayed!

18 Within this mindless vault
Lie Tristan and Isolt
Tranced in each other's beauties.
They had no other duties.

19 When I shall be without regret
And shall mortality forget,
When I shall die who lived for this,
I shall not miss the things I miss.
And you who notice where I lie
Ask not my name. It is not I.

20 I was concerned for you and keep that part
In these days, irrespective of the heart:
And not for friendship, not for love, but cast
In that role by the presence of the past.

21 Grief restrains grief as dams torrential rain,
And time grows fertile with extended pain.

22 Dear child whom I begot,
Forgive me if my page
Hymns not your helpless age,
For you are mine, and not:
Mine as sower and sown,
But in yourself your own.

Motto for a sun dial

23 I who by day am function of the light
Am constant and invariant by night.

On the Calculus

24 From almost naught to almost all I flee,
And *almost* has almost confounded me,
Zero my limit, and infinity.

25 In this child's game where you grow warm and warmer,
And new grand passions still exceed the former,
In what orgasm of high sentiment
Will you conclude and sleep at last content?

26 After some years Bohemian came to this,
This Maenad with hair down and gaping kiss
Wild on the barren edge of under fifty.
She would finance his art if he were thrifty.

27 Genius is born and made. This heel who mastered
By infinite pains his trade was born a bastard.

28 Dark thoughts are my companions. I have wined
With lewdness and with crudeness, and I find
Love is my enemy, dispassionate hate
Is my redemption though it come too late,
Though I come to it with a broken head
In the cat-house of the dishevelled dead.

History of ideas

29 God is love. Then by conversion
Love is God, and sex conversion.

30 Kiss me goodbye, to whom I've only been
Cause for uncloistered virtue, not for sin.

31 He weeps and sleeps with Dido, calls him cad
Who followed God, and finds real Didos bad.

32 Silence is noisome, but the loud logician
Raises more problems by their definition.
Then let your discourse be a murmured charm
And so ambiguous none hears its harm.

33   Hang up your weaponed wit
Who were destroyed by it.
If silence fails, then grace
Your speech with commonplace,
And studiously amaze
Your audience with his phrase.
He will commend your wit
When you abandon it.

34   Death in this music dwells. I cease to be
In this attentive, taut passivity.

35   Action is memoir: you may read my story
Even in pure thought, scandal in allegory.

36   How we desire desire! Joy of surcease
In joy's fulfilment is bewildered peace,
And harsh renewal. Life in fear of death
Will trivialize the void with hurrying breath,
With harsh indrawal. Nor love nor lust impels us.
Time's hunger to be realised compels us.

37   Dear, if unsocial privacies obsess me,
If to my exaltations I be true,
If memories and images possess me,
Yes, if I love you, what is that to you?
My folly is no passion for collusion.
I cherish my illusions as illusion.

To a Student

38 Fiction, but memoir. Here you know
Motive and act who made them so.
Life falls in scenes; its tragedies
Close in contrived catastrophes.
Much is evasion. Some years pass
With *Some years later*. In this glass
Reflection sees reflection's smile
And self-engrossment is good style.

Fiction is fiction: its one theme
Is its allegiance to its scheme.
Memoir is memoir: there your heart
Awaits the judgment of your art.
But memoir in fictitious guise
Is telling truth by telling lies.

39 This is my curse. Pompous, I pray
That you believe the things you say
And that you live them, day by day.

40 The self is terrified, shade calls to shade,
Ghost destroys ghost whose ghost springs undismayed,
And fear regresses to infinity.
I know the spell in the mythology
Of this despair, I know love's charms affright
Psychotic goblins in the Gothic night,
I know your arms. Dear, in that incantation
Despair in joy attains its consummation.

41 The scholar of theology and science
Who falls in love must in good faith affiance
Love and his trades; must prove the commonplace
Of his divine research, *Love goes by grace,*
Never by merit; judge by divination
Supernal from infernal visitation;
And risk his faith. As scientist he tries
By the inductive leap, immense surmise,
To force the future to confirm his guess,
Though predisposed toward ill or good success,
Pledged to the issue. So he may discover
As scholar truth, sincerity as lover.

42 Soft found a way to damn me undefended:
I was forgiven who had not offended.

43 This Humanist whom no beliefs constrained
Grew so broad-minded he was scatter-brained.

44 If I can't know myself it's something gained
To help my enemy to know his sin,
Especially since in him it's only feigned,
For the ideal exemplar lies within.

45 Dear, my familiar hand in love's own gesture
Gives irresponsive absence flesh and vesture.

46 Each that I loved is now my enemy
To whom I severally inscribe my journal,
Who was defrauded of my vanity,
Peeled like a grain of wheat to the white kernel.

A is A: Monism refuted

47 This Monist who reduced the swarm
Of being to a single form,
Emptying the universe for fun,
Required two A's to think them one.

Epigraph to The Judge is Fury

48 These the assizes: here the charge, denial,
Proof and disproof: the poem is the trial.
Experience is defendant, and the jury
Peers of tradition, and the judge is fury.

49 Lip was a man who used his head.
He used it when he went to bed
With his friend's wife, and with his friend,
With either sex at either end.

50 Naked I came, naked I leave the scene,
And naked was my pastime in between.

51 All in due time: love will emerge from hate,
And the due deference of truth from lies.
If not quite all things come to those who wait
They will not need them: in due time one dies.

52 Life flows to death as rivers to the sea,
    And life is fresh and death is salt to me.

53 On a cold night I came through the cold rain
    And false snow to the wind shrill on your pane
    With no hope and no anger and no fear.
    Who are you? and with whom do you sleep here?

54 And what is love? Misunderstanding, pain,
    Delusion, or retreat? It is in truth
    Like an old brandy after a long rain,
    Distinguished, and familiar, and aloof.

55 I had gone broke, and got set to come back,
    And lost, on a hot day and a fast track,
    On a long shot at long odds, a black mare
    By Hatred out of Envy by Despair.

On *Doctor Drink*

56 A reader (did he buy it, borrow, beg,
    Or read it in a bookstore on one leg?)
    Dislikes my book; calls it, to my discredit,
    A book you can't put down before you've read it.
    Yet in this paucity, this drouth of phrases,
    There are as many as in children phases:
    The trivial, vulgar, and exalted jostle
    Each other in a way to make the apostle

Of culture and right feeling shudder faintly.
It is a shudder that affects the saintly.
It is shudder by which I am faulted.
I like the trivial, vulgar and exalted.

57 Here lies my wife. Eternal peace
Be to us both with her decease.

58 My name is Ebenezer Brown.
I carted all the trash of town
For sixty years. On the last day
I trust my Lord will cart me away.

59 I married in my youth a wife.
She was my own, my very first.
She gave the best years of her life.
I hope nobody gets the worst.

60 Here lies New Critic who would fox us
With his poetic paradoxes.
Though he lies here rigid and quiet,
If he could speak he would deny it.

61 You wonder why Drab sells her love for gold?
To have the means to buy it when she's old.

62 You ask me how Contempt who claims to sleep
With every woman that has ever been
Can still maintain that women are skin deep?
They never let him any deeper in.

63 With every wife he can, and you know why?
Bold goes to bed because really he's shy.
And why I publish it none knows but I:
I publish it because really I'm shy.

64 Bride loved old words, and found her pleasure marred
On the first night, her expectations jarred,
And thirty inches short of being a yard.

65 Career was feminine, resourceful, clever.
You'd never guess to see her she felt ever
By a male world oppressed. How much they weigh!
Even her hand disturbed her as she lay.

66 Your affair, my dear, need not be a mess.
See at the next table with what finesse,
With what witty tensions and what tense wit,
As intricate as courtship, the love-fated
Sir Gawain and the Fay at lunch commit
Faithful adultery unconsummated.

67 The Elders at their services begin
With paper offerings. They release from sin
The catechumens on the couches lying
In visions, testimonies, prophesying:
Not, 'Are you saved?' they ask, but in informal
Insistent query, 'Brother, are you normal?'

68 *Arms and the man I sing*, and sing for joy,
Who was last year all elbows and a boy.

69 Another novel, and the prostitute
And the initiate. I who have never known
The rite of artistry, or how to do it,
With meager manuscript sit here alone.

70 And now you're ready who while she was here
Hung like a flag in a calm. Friend, though you stand
Erect and eager, in your eye a tear,
I will not pity you, or lend a hand.

For a College Yearbook

71 Somewhere on these bare rocks in some bare hall,
Perhaps unrecognized, wisdom and learning
Flash like a beacon on a sleeper's wall,
Ever distant and dark, ever returning.

72   Love, receive Lais' glass, the famous whore,
      In whose reflection you appear no more.

73   Friend, on this scaffold Thomas More lies dead
      Who would not cut the Body from the Head.

Night-piece

74   Three matches in a folder, you and me.
      I sit and smoke, and now there's only two,
      And one, and none: a small finality
      In a continuing world, a thing to do.
      And you, fast at your book, whose fingers keep
      Its single place as you sift down to sleep.

New York: 5 March 1957

75   Lady, of anonymous flesh and face
      In the half-light, in the rising embrace
      Of my losses, in the dark dress and booth,
      The stripper of the gawking of my youth,
      Lady, I see not, care not, what you are.
      I sit with beer and bourbon at this bar.

76   Good Fortune, when I hailed her recently,
      Passed by me with the intimacy of shame
      As one that in the dark had handled me
      And could no longer recollect my name.

77 I write you in my need. Please write
    As simply, in terms black and white,
    And do not fear hyperbole,
    Uncompromising Flattery!
    I can believe the best of me.

Love's Progress

78 Pal was her friend, her lover, and, dismissed,
    Became at last her lay psychiatrist.

79 Mistress of scenes, good-by. Your maidenhead
    Was fitter for the couch than for the bed.

On a Line from Bodenham's 'Belvedere'

80 'Experience is the mistress of old age:'
    Kept at my cost, as old as I am, bitch
    And parasite, I screw her in my rage
    And would kill her, but which of us is which?

81 Who am I? I have pondered with my peers,
    And unexisting existentially
    For years I have gone sidelong through the years
    And half faced and half assed reality.

82 Young Sensitive one summer on the Cape
    Met a Miss Splash. She led him to a rape
    Through all the jagged colours of her mood.
    It was like sleeping with an abstract nude.

    124

83   An Oedipean Mom and Dad
Made Junior Freud feel pretty bad,
And when they died he was so vexed
He never after hetrosexed.

84   Mick was a lousy lover as Americans
Are said to be, that is, the men. How could
He know, an Irish boy, the feminine's
Orgasmic concentration on her pud.

Modern Love

85   She has a husband, he a wife.
What a way to spend a life!
So whenever they are free
They synchronize adultery,
And neither one would dare to stop
Without a simultaneous plop.

86   A periphrastic insult, not a banal:
You are not a loud-mouthed and half-assed worm;
You are, sir, magni-oral, semi-anal,
A model for a prophylactic firm.

87   Cocktails at six, suburban revelry:
He in one corner with the Chest Convex,
She in another with Virility.
So they went home, had dinner, and had sex.

88   Some twenty years of marital agreement
Ended without crisis in disagreement.
What was the problem? Nothing of importance,
Nothing but money, sex, and self-importance.

89   A faint smile of distraction, moist response
At the least touch, even her husband's. Can
Imaged adultery fulfil his wants
And still be sleeping with the other man?

90   Prue loved her man: to clean, to mend,
To have a child for his sake, fuss
Over him, and on demand
Sleep with him with averted face.

91   I grow old, but I know that Science some
Few years from now will found millenium:
To be immortal, with an annual raise,
And practice continence on New Year's Days.

92   Leisure and summer vistas and life green
Within the limits of the sky. What more
Could one want if he also had a clean,
Accommodating, inexpensive whore?

Towards Tucson

93   In this attractive desolation,
A world's debris framed by a fence,
Drink is my only medication
And loneliness is my defence.

94 There is a ghost town of abandoned love
With tailings of used hope, leavings of risk,
Deserted cherishings masked with new life,
Where the once ugly is now picturesque.

Portrait

95 I am the other woman, so much other
It is no task to tell the one from tother.

On a Letter

96 Unsigned, almost unsent, and all unsaid
Except the sending, which I take as read.

For a Woman with Child

97 We are ourselves but carriers. Life
Incipient grows to separateness
And is its own meaning. Life is,
And not; there is no nothingness.

98 Old love is old resentment, novelty
Confined by expectation, ease and distance
Living together, with mute fantasy
A descant on the plainsong of persistence.

99 Illusion and delusion are that real
We segregate from real reality;
But cause and consequence locate the real:
What is not is also reality.

I00   Reader, goodbye. While my associates
        Redeem the world in moral vanity
        Or live the casuistry of an affair
        I shall go home: bourbon and beer at five,
        Some money, some prestige, some love, some sex,
        My input and my output satisfactory.

Latin Lines

DECIMUS LABERIUS

An Old Actor Addresses Julius Caesar

Necessity, the impact of whose sidelong course
Many attempt to escape and only few succeed,
Whither have you thrust down, almost to his wits' ends,
Him whom flattery, whom never bribery
Could in his youth avail to shake him from his stand?
But see how easily an old man slips, and shows,
Moved by the complacency of this most excellent man,
Calm and complaisant, a submissive, fawning speech!
Yet naught to a conqueror could the gods themselves deny,
And who then would permit one man to say him nay?
I who existed sixty long years without stain,
A Roman Knight who went from his paternal gods,
Now return home a mime. And certainly today
I've lived out one more day than I should have lived.
Fortune, unrestrained in prosperity and ill,
Were it your pleasure with the lure and praise of letters
To shatter the very summit of my good name,
Why when I prospered, when my limbs were green with youth,
When I could satisfy an audience and such a man,
Did you not bend my suppleness and spit on me?
Now you cast me? Whither? What brought I to the stage?
The ornament of beauty, dignity of flesh,
Fire of the spirit, the music of a pleasing voice?
As twining ivy kills the stout heart of the tree,
So has senility in time's embrace destroyed me,
And like a sepulchre I keep only a name.

CATULLUS 85

I hate and love her. If you ask me why
I don't know. But I feel it and am torn.

HORACE

Odes 1.9

See how resplendent in deep snow
Soracte stands, how straining trees
   Scarce can sustain their burden
     Now that the rivers congeal and freeze.

Thaw out the chill, still heaping more
Wood on the hearth; ungrudgingly
   Pour forth from Sabine flagons,
     O Thaliarchus, the ripened wine.

Leave all else to the gods. They soon
Will level on the yeasty deep
   Th' embattled tempests, stirring
     Cypress no more, nor agèd ash.

Tomorrow may no man divine.
This day that Fortune gives set down
   As profit, nor while young still
     Scorn the rewards of sweet dancing love,

So long as from your flowering days
Crabbed age delays. Now through the parks
   Soft whisperings toward nightfall
     Visit again at the trysting hour;

Now from her bower comes the charmed laugh,
Betrayer of the hiding girl;
   Now from her arm the forfeit
     Plundered, her fingers resisting not.

MARTIAL 1.32

Sabinus, I don't like you. You know why?
Sabinus, I don't like you. That is why.

MARTIAL 1.33

In private she mourns not the late-lamented;
If someone's by her tears leap forth on call.
Sorrow, my dear, is not so easily rented.
They are true tears that without witness fall.

MARTIAL 2.4

Bert is beguiling with his mother,
She is beguiling with her Bert.
They call each other *Sister*, *Brother*,
And others call them something other.
Is it no fun to be yourselves?
Or is this fun? I'd say it's not.
A mother who would be a sister
Would be no mother and no sister.

MARTIAL 2.5

Believe me, sir, I'd like to spend whole days,
Yes, and whole evenings in your company,
But the two miles between your house and mine
Are four miles when I go there to come back.
You're seldom home, and when you are deny it,
Engrossed with business or with yourself.
Now, I don't mind the two-mile trip to see you;
What I do mind is going four to not to.

MARTIAL 2.55

You would be courted, dear, and I would love you.
But be it as you will, and I will court you.
But if I court you, dear, I will not love you.

MARTIAL 2.68

That I now call you by your name
Who used to call you sir and master,
You needn't think it impudence.
I bought myself with all I had.
He ought to sir a sir and master
Who's not himself, and wants to have
Whatever sirs and masters want.
Who can get by without a slave
Can get by, too, without a master.

MARTIAL 4.33

You write, you tell me, for posterity.
May you be read, my friend, immediately.

MARTIAL 4.69

You serve the best wines always, my dear sir,
And yet they say your wines are not so good.
They say you are four times a widower.
They say . . . A drink? I don't believe I would.

STATIUS

Siluae 5.4: On Sleep

What was my crime, youthful most gentle god,
What folly was it that I alone should lack,
Sweet Sleep, thy gifts? All herds, birds, beasts are still,
The curved mountains seem wearily asleep,
Streams rage with muted noise, the sea-wave falls,
And the still-nodding deep rests on the shore.
Seven times now returning Phoebe sees
My sick eyes stare, and so the morning star
And evening, so Tithonia glides by
My tears, sprinkling sad dew from her cool whip.
How, then, may I endure? Not though were mine
The thousand eyes wherewith good Argus kept
But shifting watch, nor all his flesh awake.
But now, alas! If this long night some lover
In his girl's arms should willingly repel thee,

Thence come sweet Sleep! Nor with all thy power
Pour through my eyes—so may they ask, the many,
More happy—; touch me with thy wand's last tip,
Enough, or lightly pass with hovering step.

HADRIAN

My little soul, my vagrant charmer,
The friend and house-guest of this matter,
Where will you now be visitor
In naked pallor, little soul,
And not so witty as you were?

ST. AMBROSE

Aeterne Rerum Conditor

Builder eternally of things,
Thou rulest over night and day,
Disposing time in separate times
That Thou mayst lessen weariness;

Now crows the herald of the day,
Watchful throughout the wasting dark,
To walkers in the night a clock
Marking the hours of dark and dawn.

The morning star arises now
To free the obscure firmament;
Now every gang and prowling doom
Forsakes the dark highways of harm.

The sailor now regathers strength,
The channels of the sea grow calm;
And now Peter, the living rock,
Washes his guilt in the last crow.

Then quickly let us rise and go;
The cock stirs up the sleepy-head,
And chides again the lie-a-bed;
The cock convicts them who deny.

And to cock-crow our hopes reply;
Thy grace refills our ailing hearts;
The sword of brigandage is hid;
And faith returns where faith had fled.

Jesu, look back on us who fall,
Straighten the conduct of our life;
If Thou lookst back, denials fail,
And guilt is melted in a tear.

Thou Light, illumine with Thy light
Our sleeping lethargy of soul;
Thy name the first our lips shall choose,
Discharging thus our vows to Thee.

THE ARCHPOET

The Confession of Bishop Golias

Inwardly fired with vehement wrath,
In bitterness I will speak my mind;
Made of material light as lath,
I am like a leaf tossed by the wind.

137

Though it were just for the wise and brave
To place their seat on the rock of will,
Fool, I am like the flowing wave
That under one sky is ever unstill.

I am borne on as a pilotless ship,
As a vagrant bird through the cloudy haze;
Ungoverned by reins, ungoverned by whip,
I gad with my kind, I follow their ways.

I walk the broad path in the fashion of youth,
Forgetful of virtue, entangled with sin;
Avid of pleasure more than of truth
I die in soul but take care of my skin.

Most worthy prelate, I pray your pardon,
I die a good death, swing on a sweet rope,
At sight of the ladies I still get a hard on,
Whom I cannot by touch, I sin with in hope.

Who placed on a pyre will not burn in the fire?
Or dallying at Pavia can keep himself chaste?
Where Venus goes hunting young men for hire,
Drooping her eyelids and fixing her face.

Hippolytus placed in Pavia today
Would not be Hippolytus 'when the dawn came';
To the bedroom of Venus still runs the broad way,
Nor in all those towers is the tower of shame.

Again, I'm charged with playing strip poker:
When play casts me out in my naked skin,
Shivering, I sweat while my mind plays stoker,
And I write better verse than I did within.

The tavern, thirdly, I note in this summing
Up of the life I will ever have led
Till I hear the holy angels coming,
Singing rest eternal unto the dead;

For I propose in the tavern to die
That wine may be near when the throat grows hard,
And the chorus of angels may joyfully cry,
'O Lord, be kindly to this drunkard.'

The lamp of the soul is lighted by wine,
Sotted with nectar it flies to the sky;
Wine of the tavern is far more divine
Than watery wine that the priest raises high.

They say a poet should flee public places
And choose his seat in a quiet retreat:
He sweats, presses on, stays awake, and erases,
Yet comes back with scarcely one clear conceit.

The chorus of poets should fast and abstain,
Avoid public quarrels and brawls with their neighbours:
That they may compose what will ever remain,
They die in a cell, overcome by their labours.

Nature to such gives a suitable crown:
I never could write on an empty purse;
Myself when fasting a boy could knock down;
Thirsting and hunger I hate like a hearse.

Never's the spirit of poetry given
Except when the belly is fat and sleek;
While Bacchus is lord of my cerebral heaven,
Apollo moves through me and marvels I speak.

Behold, of my vice I was that informer
By whom your henchmen indicted me;
No one of them is his own accuser,
Though he hopes to sport through eternity.

So I stand before the blessed prelate
Urging that precept of our Lord wherein
He casts the first stone, nor spares the poet,
Whose heart is wholly devoid of sin.

I've charged myself with whatever I knew
And vomited up my long cherished dole;
The old life passes, gives way to the new;
Man notes appearance, Jove sees the soul.

Primate of Cologne, grant me your blessing,
Absolve the sinner who begs your grace;
Impose due penance on him confessing;
Whatever you bid I'll gladly embrace.

BEMBO

On Raphael

This is that Raphael the Great Source of All
Feared as Its master, with his fall to fall.

JANUS VITALIS PANORMITANUS

Rome

You that a stranger in mid-Rome seek Rome
And can find nothing in mid-Rome of Rome,
Behold this mass of walls, these abrupt rocks,
Where the vast theatre lies overwhelmed.
Here, here is Rome! Look how the very corpse
Of greatness still imperiously breathes threats!
The world she conquered, strove herself to conquer,
Conquered that nothing be unconquered by her.
Now conqueror Rome's interred in conquered Rome,
And the same Rome conquered and conqueror.
Still Tiber stays, witness of Roman fame,
Still Tiber flows on swift waves to the sea.
Learn hence what Fortune can: the unmoved falls
And the ever-moving will remain forever.

MORE

The Astrologer

What is it, fool, in the tall stars you'd find
About the earthy morals of your spouse?
Why search so far? Your fears are close at hand.
For while you polled the poles for what she'd do
She did it willingly and on the ground.

BUCHANAN

The Pope from penance purgatorial
Freed some, but Martin Luther freed them all.

BUCHANAN

Neaera when I'm there is adamant,
And when I'm not there is annoyed,
And not from tenderness and sentiment
But that my pain is unenjoyed.

BUCHANAN

Rome conquered earth with arms, the sea with ships,
Till the world's limits were the city limits.
Only the otherworlds remained. The faith
Of the first Pontiffs shattered old Olympus,
And their posterity, adventurous
As they, hasten to Hell in hotfoot haste.